Make it Grow!

Written by:
Anna Claybourne

Illustrated by:
Kimberley Scott and Venetia Dean

First published in 2013 by Wayland
Copyright © Wayland 2013

Wayland
338 Euston Road
London NW1 3BH

Wayland Australia
Hachette Children's Books
Level 17/207
Kent Street
Sydney, NSW 2000

Senior Editor: Julia Adams
Editor: Annabel Stones
Designer: Anthony Hannant (LittleRedAnt)
Illustrator (step-by-steps): Kimberley Scott
Illustrator (incidentals and final crafts): Venetia Dean
Proofreader & Indexer: Sara Harper

The website addresses (URLs) included in this book were valid at the time of going to press. However, it is possible that contents or addresses may have changed since the publication of this book. No responsibility for any such changes can be accepted by either the author or the Publisher.

Dewey categorisation: 571.8

ISBN 978 0 7502 7736 5

Printed in China

Wayland is a division of Hachette Children's Books,
an Hachette UK company.

www.hachette.co.uk

Picture acknowledgements:
All photographs: Shutterstock

Contents

Bigger and BIGGER!

We're surrounded all the time by things that are growing and changing. Living things, such as plants, trees and animals all grow. You are a living thing too, and you are also growing.

4

LIKE WHAT?

Non-living things, such as crystals and clouds, can also grow. And although you may not always notice it, any substance can get bigger or smaller, depending on how hot or cold it is. In fact, there's hardly anything that stays the same size! Here are some examples:

- Storm clouds get bigger and change shape.

- A baby grows into a child, then an adult.

- Plants don't just grow taller, they also grow new buds, leaves or flowers every year.

- Air grows and takes up more space when it gets hotter.

TEST IT OUT

The activities in this book let you explore how things grow, and the different reasons why they do. You can experiment with plants, crystals, ice, hot air, and even try out some expanding food recipes that you can eat afterwards!

Rocks and minerals can grow in the form of crystals, stalactites and stalagmites.

JUICY!

DRIP, DRIP

WHAT SCIENTISTS DO

When you do science experiments, you are finding out how the world works, just like a real scientist. To do it right, follow these real-life science tips:

- Always follow the instructions and watch what happens carefully.

- Write down the results to keep a record of them. You can also take photos or make sketches.

- If possible, do experiments a few times over to check they always work.

Egg~head

Real hair grows, and so does this cress hair! Use it to make yourself a green-haired egg-head. You will need an adult to help you with the egg-boiling part.

YOU WILL NEED
1) A fresh egg
2) A saucepan
3) A cooker
4) Water
5) Felt-tip pens
6) Kitchen paper
7) Cotton wool
8) Cress seeds

Here's What to Do...

1. Ask an adult to hard-boil the egg and let it cool. Then slice the top off, eat (or throw away) the egg and carefully wash out and dry the shell.

2. Draw a face on your eggshell.

3. Put a piece of wet kitchen paper in the bottom of the shell, and a ball of wet cotton wool on top.

4. Sprinkle cress seeds onto the cotton wool. Stand it in a warm, sunny place such as a windowsill.

It will take a couple of days, but your cress seeds should start to sprout and grow. They don't need soil, just water, warmth and light. Seeds can sense when they have the things they need to grow, and this makes them start to sprout, or germinate.

A seed sends roots down into the soil and a shoot grows upwards.

TROUBLESHOOTER

To help your egg-head stand up, you can sit it in an eggcup or egg box, or on top of a toilet roll tube.

If you don't want to use an egg, a small yoghurt pot or plant pot works too.

TIME FOR LUNCH!

When the cress has grown, you can eat it (unlike real hair!). Snip it off at the bottoms of the stalks, wash it, and put it in a salad or an egg or cheese sandwich.

WHAT NEXT?

You can keep your cress head extra warm and damp by covering it with a mini 'greenhouse' made of an upside-down clear plastic bowl.

Growing Beans

A seed contains all the information it needs to grow into a plant, as long as it gets the right things. What will make it keep growing? Runner bean or green bean seeds are best for this.

YOU WILL NEED

1) Two empty glass jam jars
2) Runner bean or green bean seeds from a garden centre
3) Kitchen paper
4) Water
5) A large cardboard box with lid flaps

Here's What to Do...

1. Line each jar with a piece of kitchen paper, curving it around the inside like this.

2. Push two beans halfway down inside each jar between the glass and the paper.

3. Add about 4 cm of water to each jar, making sure it touches the bottom of the kitchen paper.

4. Leave one jar on a sunny windowsill. Put the other next to it, but inside a cardboard box with the lid flaps closed.

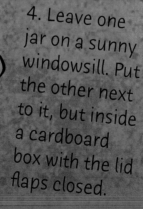

5. Check every day to see what's happening!

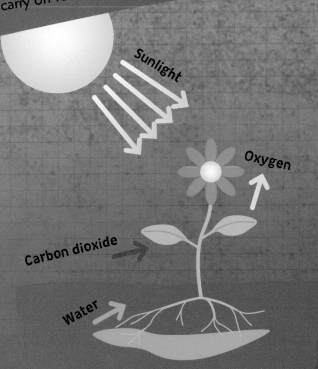

WHAT'S GOING ON?

The seeds should germinate and sprout a stalk and a root. But to keep growing bigger and bigger, plants need light, so the one in the dark may not do as well.

TROUBLESHOOTER

To stop the paper and seeds from drying out, top up the water level each day.

WHY DO PLANTS NEED LIGHT?

Plants grow by turning water and carbon dioxide gas from the air into sugary food. This process, called photosynthesis, uses energy. Plants get this energy by taking in light through their leaves. A seed can start to grow using food energy stored inside it, but can't carry on for long without light.

Sunlight

Oxygen

Carbon dioxide

Water

WHAT NEXT?

A bean seed that's growing well can be moved into a pot of soil and then planted in a sunny place or container outdoors. With luck you should be able to grow beans to eat.

supermarket sprout

You might have noticed vegetables in your fridge or cupboards starting to 'sprout' when they get a bit old. This experiment lets you take a closer look at what happens. Compare non-organic vegetables with organic ones, to see if there's a difference.

Here's What to Do...

YOU WILL NEED
1) Organic and non-organic potatoes, onions and carrots
2) An empty egg box
3) Small glasses, jars and saucers
4) Water

1. To sprout the potatoes, simply choose smallish ones and sit them in an egg box.

2. Stand each onion in a narrow glass with water reaching up to their undersides.

3. Ask an adult to cut off the thick ends of the carrots and stand them in saucers of water.

4. Leave all your vegetables in a sunny place, and check every day to see what happens.

WHAT'S GOING ON?

Many vegetables are the root, bulb or seed part of the plant they come from. These parts can start to grow into a new plant. Look at the various ways they start to sprout out new plant parts. Non-organic ones may be slower to sprout, as they are sometimes sprayed with chemicals to stop them from sprouting in your fridge.

You can plant a well-sprouted potato in a tub of compost, water it, and keep covering the shoots with more soil as they grow. Eventually you'll have a potato plant and lots more potatoes!

! TROUBLESHOOTER

Mark the organic vegetables with labels or a pen, so you can tell them from the non-organic vegetables.

The sprouting parts on a potato are called 'eyes'.

WHAT NEXT?

If you have any home-grown vegetables, try them too.

Black bag balloon

Make a simple black bin bag grow and float! For this to work well, you need to do it outdoors, on a hot, sunny day.

Here's What to Do...

1. Open up your bin bag and shake it out to almost fill it with air.

YOU WILL NEED

1) A large black bin bag, as lightweight as possible

2) Strong sewing thread

2. Tie the opening tightly closed, and tie on a long piece of thread.

3. Take the bag out into bright sunshine and tie the other end of the thread to something secure, like a bench or railings.

4. Wait for the bag to warm up. What happens?

12

WHAT'S GOING ON?

Most substances expand, or grow, as they get warmer. The sun heats up the bag and this warms the air inside. As it gets hotter, the air molecules move around more, and push away from each other harder, taking up more space. The air in the bag is now less dense than the cooler air around it, and the bag starts to float upwards. Black absorbs more sunlight than other colours, which helps warm the bag.

Cold air

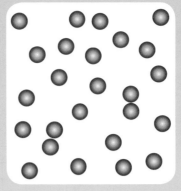

Warm air

HEAT IS MOVEMENT

As a substance gets hotter, it takes in energy. The extra energy makes the molecules move about more and faster. That's what heat is!

A hot-air balloon works in exactly the same way.

TROUBLESHOOTER

If you don't have warm sunshine, you can do the experiment indoors and heat up the bag with a hairdryer. Ask an adult to help.

WHAT NEXT?

You can buy even bigger flying black balloons, often called solar balloons, in toy shops. Or you could try making a bigger one by taping several bin bags together into a long sausage.

Make a thermometer

Heat can make things expand, so thermometers can measure heat by measuring how much things grow. This simple bottle thermometer is easy to make.

YOU WILL NEED

1) A small, clear plastic drink bottle
2) Water
3) Bright food colouring
4) A long, clear plastic straw
5) Modelling clay

Here's What to Do...

1. Half-fill the bottle with water and add a few drops of food colouring to make it easy to see.

RED

2. Take a lump of modelling clay and wrap it around a straw, towards one end.

3. Stick the long end of the straw into the bottle, right into the water, and seal the modelling clay around the bottle neck.

4. Put your hands around the top of bottle to warm it up, or leave in a warm place, such as on a radiator.

14

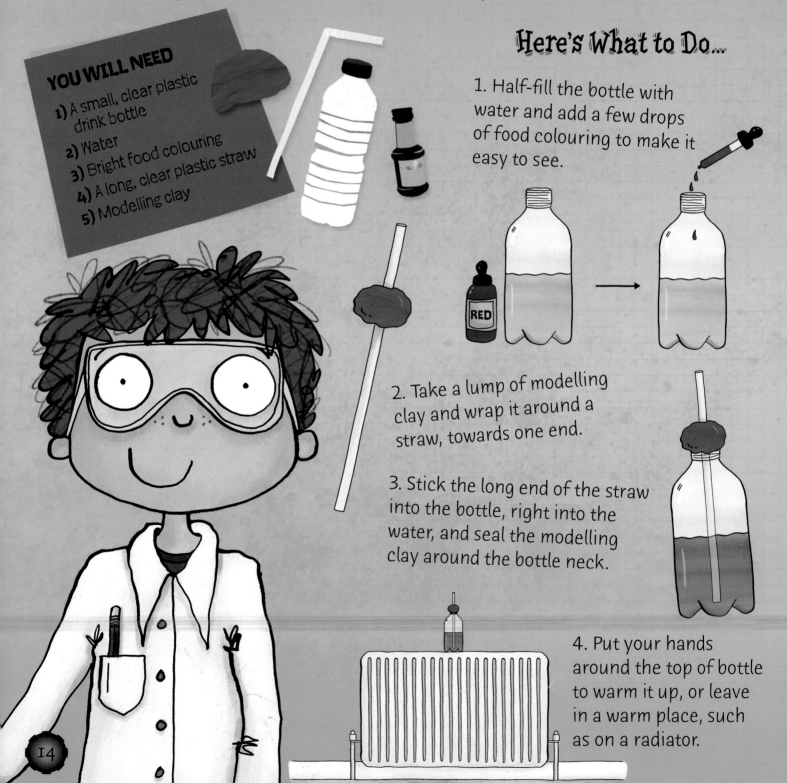

WHAT'S GOING ON?

As you warm the bottle, the air inside it warms up and expands. This pushes the liquid inside the bottle down, and it rises up inside the straw. If you let the bottle cool down, the level will fall again.

!

TROUBLESHOOTER

The modelling clay must be tightly sealed around the bottle and the straw with no gaps.

EVERYTHING EXPANDS

The liquid in the bottle also expands as it warms us, but this is hard to see because liquids don't expand as much as gases do. This thermometer uses a liquid that is sensitive to temperature changes and a very thin tube, so that you can see the change in liquid level easily.

WHAT NEXT?

Tape a small piece of card to the straw, so you can mark on a temperature scale for different levels. You could use an existing thermometer to measure the temperature indoors and outdoors, then mark these levels on your own version.

Expanding ice

Most substances expand when they get warmer, and shrink, or contract, when they get cooler. When water freezes, though, something different happens – because water is actually very unusual.

YOU WILL NEED

1) Two small plastic drink bottles
2) Water
3) A fridge-freezer

Here's What to Do...

1. Carefully fill both bottles with cold water right to the brim. Don't put the lids on.

2. Stand one bottle in the fridge, and the other one in the freezer, and leave them overnight.

3. Check them in the morning. What's happened?

Water molecules   Hydrogen bonds

WHAT'S GOING ON?

When water freezes, it gets colder, so you would expect it to shrink. Actually, it expands and gets bigger, making it poke out of the top of the bottle. This happens because as liquid water becomes solid ice, the molecules form a fixed grid or lattice pattern. This pushes them away from each other, so the ice takes up more space.

Icebergs and ice cubes float because they take up more space than water, and weigh less for their size.

TROUBLESHOOTER

The bottles must be completely upright. If this is tricky, stand them on a flat, hard surface like a chopping board.

WHAT NEXT?

Take an ice cube and float it in a small bowl of water. Top up the water in the bowl until it's full to the brim. Let the ice melt. What will happen? Although the ice sticks up out of the water to start with, it doesn't make the bowl overflow when it melts, because the water contracts back to its previous size.

Sugary strings

Some substances will grow into regular-shaped crystals if they have a chance. You can make these crystal strings from sugar. Take care, and ask an adult to do the cooking for you.

YOU WILL NEED

1) A saucepan
2) Water
3) A measuring cup
4) Caster sugar
5) A wooden spoon
6) A pencil
7) String
8) Scissors
9) A clear, clean glass jam jar

Here's What to Do...

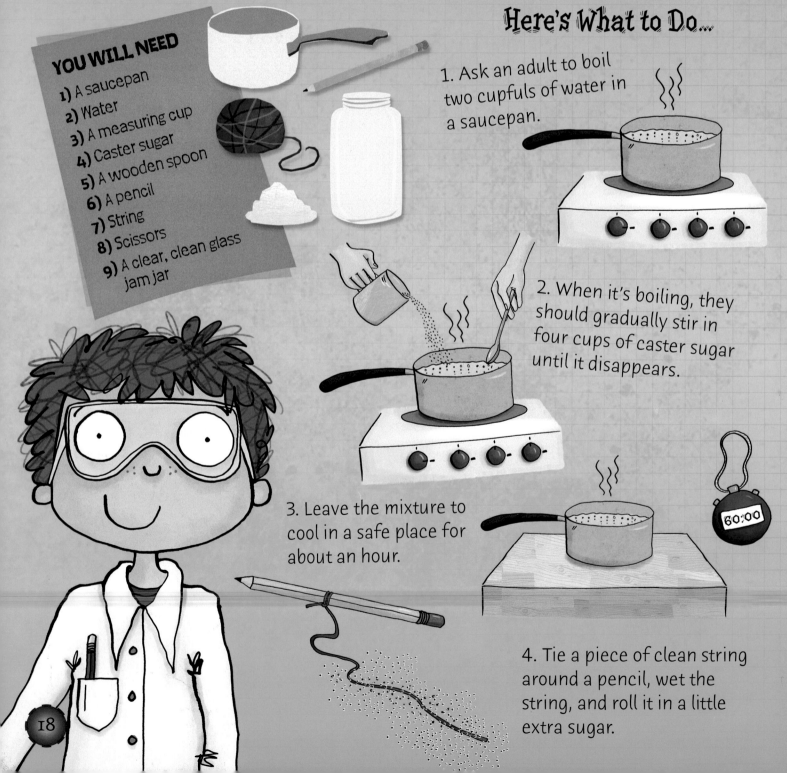

1. Ask an adult to boil two cupfuls of water in a saucepan.

2. When it's boiling, they should gradually stir in four cups of caster sugar until it disappears.

3. Leave the mixture to cool in a safe place for about an hour.

4. Tie a piece of clean string around a pencil, wet the string, and roll it in a little extra sugar.

5. Fill the jar with your cooled sugar solution.

6. Place the pencil over the jar so the string dangles into the liquid. Leave in a safe, cool place for a few days.

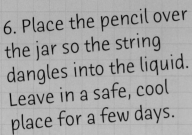

WHAT'S GOING ON?

Slowly, sugar crystals should start to grow on your string. If you leave it a full week, you should have a large clump of crystals on the string when you lift it out. Crystals form as a substance dissolved in a liquid finds a surface to stick to, and more and more of it attaches itself to the surface.

CRYSTALS IN NATURE

Many substances naturally form crystals, including sugar and salt, and various types of precious stones.

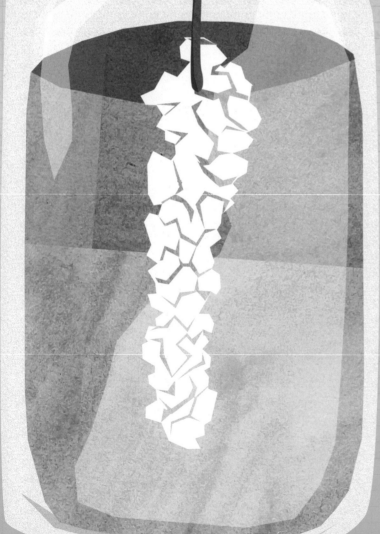

WHAT NEXT?

Make coloured crystals by stirring in a few drops of bright food colouring into the mixture after it has cooled.

Grow your own stalactites

Stalactites grow downwards from the ceiling inside caves, as water containing dissolved minerals drips from the roof. Here's how to make your own mini version.

YOU WILL NEED

1) Two jam jars
2) Hot tap water
3) Bicarbonate of soda
4) A teaspoon
5) Knitting wool or yarn
6) Two large paperclips
7) A saucer

Here's What to Do...

1. Fill both jars with hot tap water. Add several spoonfuls of bicarbonate of soda into each one, and stir until it dissolves.

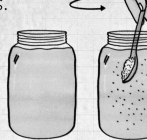

2. Take about 120 cm of yarn and fold it into four. Twist it into a single strand, and clip a paperclip onto each end.

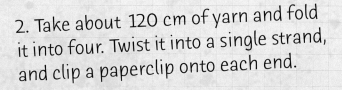

3. Put the two ends of the twisted yarn into the two jars of soda solution, using the clips to weigh them down.

4. Position the jars so that the yarn dips down in the middle, and put a saucer underneath the dip.

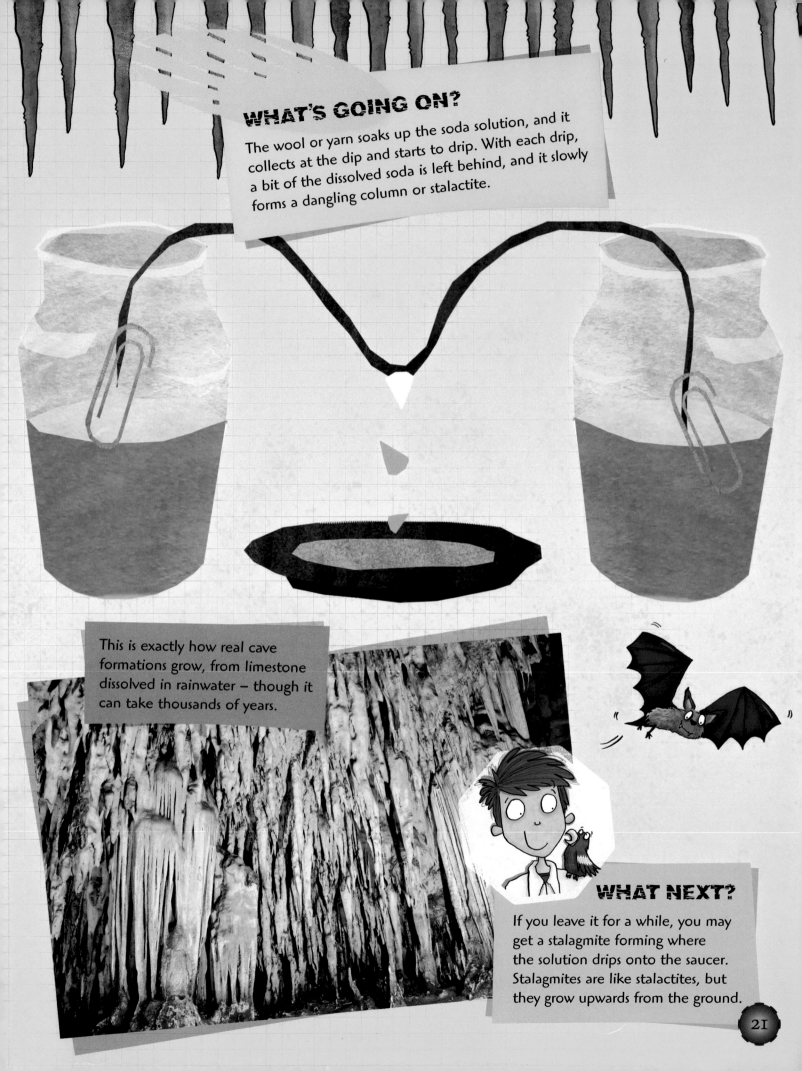

WHAT'S GOING ON?

The wool or yarn soaks up the soda solution, and it collects at the dip and starts to drip. With each drip, a bit of the dissolved soda is left behind, and it slowly forms a dangling column or stalactite.

This is exactly how real cave formations grow, from limestone dissolved in rainwater – though it can take thousands of years.

WHAT NEXT?

If you leave it for a while, you may get a stalagmite forming where the solution drips onto the saucer. Stalagmites are like stalactites, but they grow upwards from the ground.

Microwave
a marshmallow

What happens if you microwave a marshmallow? Can you guess? You'll need an adult to supervise, and make sure you don't cook the marshmallow for too long.

Here's What to Do...

YOU WILL NEED
1) Marshmallows
2) A flat microwaveable plate
3) A microwave oven

1. Sit a marshmallow on the plate.

2. Put it in the microwave, and heat on normal power for 10 seconds.

3. If not much happened, try an extra 5 or 10 seconds. Don't go above 20 seconds in all, or it could burn.

4. Compare a microwaved marshmallow with an uncooked one. How much bigger did it grow?

WHAT'S GOING ON?

A marshmallow is made of gooey sugar filled with tiny air holes – a bit like a foam cushion. When you heat it, the air in the holes expands. At the same time, the heat starts to melt and soften the sugar, making it more stretchy, and the marshmallow grows and grows.

TROUBLESHOOTER

It will work best if your marshmallow is nice and fresh out of the bag.

SAFETY WARNING

DON'T try to eat a marshmallow fresh out of the microwave – let it cool first!

YUM!

You can make a sweet snack by microwaving a marshmallow for 15-20 seconds on a small cookie, with a bit of chocolate on top.

WHAT NEXT?

What happens to the marshmallow as it cools down? (Once it's cool, you can eat it.)

Try cutting or tearing it open to see what's happened inside.

Popcorn!

Why does popcorn suddenly pop and get so much bigger when you heat it up? You'll need an adult to help you.

YOU WILL NEED

1) Popcorn kernels
2) A microwaveable plate
3) A microwave oven
4) A sewing needle

Here's What to Do...

1. Put a few popcorn kernels on the plate and put them in the microwave.

2. Switch on the power and wait for them to pop! How long do they take?

3. Now ask an adult to take some new kernels and carefully make a few holes in each one with a pin or needle.

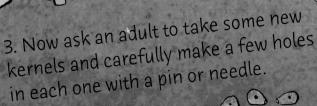

4. Try microwaving the kernels with holes in them. What happens?

WHAT'S GOING ON?

A popcorn kernel is tightly packed with cereal and water, inside a tough skin. When you heat it, the water heats, boils and makes steam, which expands. When the pressure is strong enough – POP! – the kernel explodes and the starch expands into soft, fluffy popcorn.

If a kernel has holes in its skin, they let the steam out, so it's much harder for the popcorn to pop.

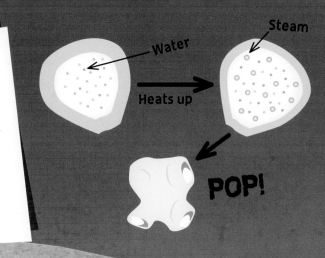

Water
Steam
Heats up
POP!

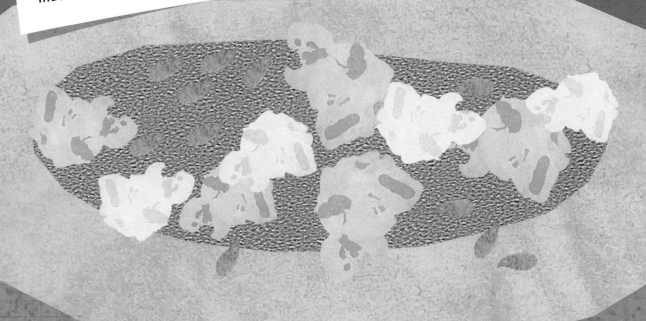

POPPED AND PUFFED

Other seeds and grains can also be popped or 'puffed' – that's how puffed rice and wheat breakfast cereals are made.

! TROUBLESHOOTER

If you don't have a microwave, you can use a saucepan on a stove with a little oil in it.

WHAT NEXT?

Can you film popcorn popping and slow it down to see what happens?

Make bread rise

Look closely at a slice of bread, and you'll see it's full of little squashy bubbles. How do they get in there? To find out, try making some bread yourself.

YOU WILL NEED

1) A large mixing bowl
2) A wooden spoon
3) A teaspoon
4) A clean worktop
5) A baking tray
6) Clingfilm
7) An oven
8) 500g bread flour (also called 'strong' flour), plus a bit extra
9) Half a teaspoon of dried yeast
10) A teaspoon of salt
11) Olive or sunflower oil
12) 300ml warm water
13) An adult to help you

Here's What to Do...

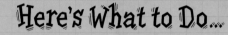

1. Mix the flour, yeast, salt, sugar, warm water and 3 teaspoons of oil in a large bowl, until they form a sticky dough.

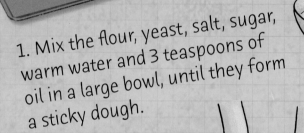

2. Sprinkle some extra flour on the table, and tip the dough onto it. Knead the dough with your hands by folding it, squashing it down, and turning it around, for about 10 minutes.

3. Put the dough back in the bowl, cover it with clingfilm, and leave it somewhere safe and warm.

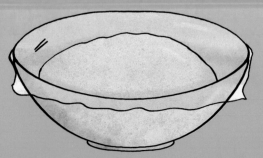

4. After an hour, it should be much bigger! Take it out, knead it again, then form it into small rolls or other shapes.

5. Rub the baking tray with a little oil and put your bread shapes on it, widely spaced out. Leave them for another hour.

WHAT'S GOING ON?

The dough grows, or 'rises', because of the yeast. Yeast is a fungus, a living thing related to mushrooms. If it has water, sugar and warmth, the yeast cells multiply and grow, and give out carbon dioxide gas. The gas bubbles get trapped and expand inside the dough, making it rise.

6. They will have grown again! Now you can ask an adult to bake them in a hot oven, at 200°C/400°F/Gas Mark 6, for about 10 minutes. Leave them to cool before eating.

! TROUBLESHOOTER

The water, and the place you leave the dough, should be medium warm, not very hot or very cold.

WHAT NEXT?

Try making a small amount of dough with no yeast in it to see what happens.

squirty cream challenge

Your challenge is to create a pile of squirty cream that's bigger than the squirty cream can! On your marks, get set.... GO!

YOU WILL NEED

1) A chilled, unopened can of squirty cream (also called instant whipped cream)

2) A large, clean serving dish or tray

Here's What to Do...

1. Take your can of squirty cream and shake it well.

2. Open it, turn it upside down and start squirting onto the dish or tray as fast as you can.

3. Try to create a tube-shaped pile of cream that's the same size and shape as the can. You could do this horizontally or vertically.

?

4. Then see if you can make it a bit bigger!

WHAT'S GOING ON?

How can more cream come out of the can than was in the can? A squirty cream can contains normal, runny liquid cream, mixed with a gas, nitrous oxide. When it's in the can, the gas is held under pressure – it's squeezed together and doesn't take up much space. But as soon as it escapes from the can, the gas expands, making bubbles and creating thick, foamy whipped cream. In fact, if you squirted all the cream out, it would grow to at least three times the size of the can.

TROUBLESHOOTER

Remember the can will only squirt well when held completely upside-down.

This shaving foam works the same way but you can't eat it!

FRUIT SALAD

If you don't want your cream to go to waste, do this experiment after dinner, then eat the cream with fresh fruit salad for pudding.

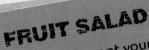

Don't worry if it falls over!

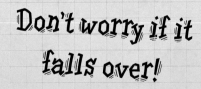

WHAT NEXT?

If you can resist eating your cream, wait several minutes and see what happens to it. You could even video it and speed it up afterwards. Does it get smaller again?

Glossary

carbon dioxide A type of gas which is present in air.

contract To get smaller.

crystal A solid substance with a naturally regular shape.

density How heavy a substance is compared to the space it takes up.

dissolve To become mixed into a liquid and broken down into tiny parts.

energy The power to do work or make things happen.

expand To get bigger.

fungi A group of living things that includes moulds and mushrooms.

gas A substance in which molecules float around freely.

germinate To start to sprout and grow.

lattice A grid-like structure with spaces in between.

limestone A type of rock that often forms caves.

mineral A naturally existing, pure, solid substance.

molecules Groups of atoms that make up substances.

nitrous oxide A type of gas.

organic Grown without using artificial fertilizers or chemical sprays.

stalactite Rock formation shaped like a pillar hanging from a cave ceiling.

stalagmite Rock formation shaped like a pillar rising from a cave floor.

further reading

BOOKS

Experiments with Plants
by Christine Taylor-Butler, Raintree, 2011

Hot Stuff: The Science of Heat and Cold
by Jay Hawkins, Windmill Books, 2013

The Science in: A Loaf of Bread
by Andrew Solway, Franklin Watts, 2008

WEBSITES

Science Kids: Plants
http://www.sciencekids.co.nz/plants.html

Exploratorium Science of Cooking: Bread
http://www.exploratorium.edu/cooking/
bread/index.html

BrainPop: Crystals
http://www.brainpop.com/science/
theearthsystem/crystals/preview.weml

Index

Whizzy SCIENCE

Titles in the series:

Make it Zoom!
978 0 7502 7732 7

Zooming cars
Straw shooter
Heli-zoomer
Zero-gravity water squirt
Zooming balloon rocket
Magazine tug-of-war
Jelly slide
Flying bucket
Whirling wind speed meter
Ping pong flinger
Gas-fuelled rocket
Magnet power

Make it Bang!
978 0 7502 7731 0

See a bang
Bang, twang, pop!
How a bang travels
The speed of a bang
Bangs and whispers
The screaming cup
High and low
The sounds of speech
Solid sounds
Stop that banging!
Find the bang
How musical are you?

Make it Change!
978 0 7502 7734 1

Turn a penny green!
Lava volcano
The red cabbage test
Exploding drinks
Make salt disappear
  and reappear
Rubbery bones
Bottle balloon
Magic ice cubes
Plastic bag ice cream
Pure water still
Make your own butter
Mould garden

Make it Grow!
978 0 7502 7736 5

Egg-head!
Growing beans
Supermarket sprout!
Black bag balloon
Make a thermometer
Expanding ice
Sugary strings
Grow your own stalactites
Microwave a marshmallow
Popcorn!
Make bread rise
Squirty cream challenge

Make it Glow!
978 0 7502 7733 4

Light and shadows
Periscope
Tea light lanterns
Make an indoor rainbow
Glowing envelopes, plasters
  and sweets!
Glow-in-the-dark shapes
Make a glowing jar lantern
Glow stick photos
Glowing water stream
Laser jelly
Camera obscura
Ultraviolet glow

Make it Splash!
978 0 7502 7735 8

Make a splash
Stretchy water skin
Upside-down cup
Water balloon pop!
Things that float
Rising raisins
Magic liquid levels
Melted crayon art
The saliva test
Make your own river
Strange gloop
More water fun